1 MONTH OF FREE READING

at

www.ForgottenBooks.com

By purchasing this book you are eligible for one month membership to ForgottenBooks.com, giving you unlimited access to our entire collection of over 1,000,000 titles via our web site and mobile apps.

To claim your free month visit:

www.forgottenbooks.com/free908148

ISBN 978-0-266-90883-8
PIBN 10908148

Forgotten Books is a registered trademark of FB &c Ltd.
Copyright © 2018 FB &c Ltd.
FB &c Ltd, Dalton House, 60 Windsor Avenue, London, SW19 2RR.
Company number 08720141. Registered in England and Wales.

For support please visit www.forgottenbooks.com

Iss. Two, Vol. 107, Winter 2005

Inside

Cover photo: University of Nevada, Reno Interim President Dr. Joe Crowley speaks at a press conference at Morrill Hall announcing his decision to replace former President John Lilley Monday, Nov. 21.
Photo by David Calvert

Left: Nevada's **Lindsay Holda** during the Wolf Pack's first round victory over the Idaho Vandals during the Western Athletic Conference tournament, Thursday, Nov. 24 at Lawlor Events Center.
Photo by David Calvert

Editor: David Calvert

Page Design: Laura Licari

Web Design: Matt Fiske

Staff Photographers: Kevin Clifford, Ben Ragains, Kelci McIntosh and Nathan Slinker

Staff Writer: Monika Mala

Special thanks to: ASUN Advisor Amy Koeckes, ASUN Executive Vice President Matt McKnight, the ASUN Publications Board, ASUN Advertising, the Reynolds School of Journalism, Ira Gostin and the Nevada Sagebrush staff

artemisia
a photo magazine for the University of Nevada, Reno

The road ahead

Above: University of Nevada, Reno graduates are silhouetted against a Nevada banner during the 2005 winter commencement ceremonies at Lawlor Events Center, Saturday, Dec. 10. Left: Nina Mazzola, a human resource management graduate hugs Dr. Yvonne Stedham after walking the stage at Lawlor Events Center. UNR issued 1034 bachelors degrees and 433 advanced diplomas.

Photos by Kevin Clifford

One thousand four hundred and sixty-seven graduates sat inside Lawlor Events Center during the 2005 winter commencement ceremony, Saturday, Dec. 10 waiting to walk. With much of its formal education behind them, one by one, the class of 2005 walked across the stage and into its next adventure. The future may be different for each graduate but the members of the winter class of 2005 do have one thing in common, the right to call themselves University of Nevada, Reno alumni.

"Graduating means four years of hard work is finally complete," said Nicole Hankins, a nursing major. "I am ready to start my career—and make money of course—but college was a lot of fun. I had a great social life through all of the different organizations I was involved with. The academic part was tough but over all, it was fun too. I am scared though," Hankins added. "There is still a lot for me to learn."

Photos by Kevin Clifford; story by Monika Mala

It means Merry Christmas, and after a week of **Hawaiian sun** and hospitality that's exactly what it was. Under the lights of Aloha Stadium in Honolulu, the Nevada Wolf Pack defeated the Central Florida **Golden Knights 49-48** in overtime on Christmas Eve. The overtime, back-and-forth-victory was the best Christmas present Nevada coach Chris Ault could ask for—**his first bowl win**—and for Nevada fans, the Sheraton Hawai'i Bowl victory capped the Pack's best season (9-3; Western Athletic Conference co-champions) since **1996.**

"We knew it was going to be a hard fight," running back Robert Hubbard said. "The guys just never gave up and we survived. We had an amazing comeback. It's a Cinderella season for us."

But the week was more than just football. As part of the festivities the Pack attended luaus, a water park, spent time on the beach and visited the U.S.S. Arizona Memorial at Pearl Harbor.

"This bowl week is something I'll remember the rest of my life," senior co-captain Adam Kiefer said.

Clockwise from above: Nevada head coach Chris Ault speaks with the media following practice, Wednesday, Dec. 21. A Polynesian fire dancer licks fire during a luau at the Royal Hawaiian Hotel in Waikiki, Tuesday, Dec. 20. Nevada's **B.J.** Mitchell runs for a first down against UCF. Mitchell was the games most valuable player finishing with 178 yards and two touchdowns. Nevada's **P.J.** Hoeper flies down a water slide at Hawaiian Adventures Water Park in Kapolei, Hawaii, Monday, Dec. 19. The U.S.S. Arizona Memorial at Pearl Harbor in Honolulu, Wednesday, Dec. 21. Adam Kiefer and Jamaal Jackson sign autographs for children at a local Shriner's Hospital in Downtown Honolulu, Thursday, Dec. 22.

a

Photos by David Calvert

Clockwise from right: Nevada's Erika Ryan, **Tristin** Johnson and Christine Harms react to an officials call during the Wolf Pack's semifinals loss to Hawaii, Friday, Nov. 25. Nevada's Salaia **Salave'a** congratulates her teammates after a point against Hawaii. Nevada's **Salave'a** and Dana Henry celebrate a point against Hawaii in the Western Athletic Conference volleyball championship

Clockwise from below: **Nevda** players gather before their first round match-up against the Idaho Vandals, Nov. 24. **Nevada head coach,** Devin Scruggs on the sidelines during the Western Athletic Conference volleyball championships. Nevada lost to Hawaii in the semifinals, but still managed an at large to the NCAA tournament. **Kristin Davis** talks with her teammates before the start of the WAC tournament.

Despite the team's success, Nevada has one hurdle it just can't clear—the Hawaii Rainbow Wahine. Nevada faced the 'Bows in the semifinals of the Western Athletic Conference tournament, Nov. 25, at Lawlor Events Center. Hawaii took the match **3-1,** despite Nevada's second game victory and advanced to the **final** round where the top-seeded Wahine beat the second seed Utah State to **win** its **fifth** consecutive conference title. **On** Thanksgiving, **a day earlier,** The Wolf Pack defeated the Idaho Vandals **3-2.**

In the loss, Nevada senior Salaia Salave'a led five Nevada players in double figures with a match high 20 kills. Carly Sorensen(16), Karly Sipherd (12), Erika Ryan (10), and Allison Hernandez (10) also reached double figures. On defense, libero Christine Harms had 16 digs, Lindsay Holda added 10 and freshman Dana Henry had 12. Setter Tristin Johnson had 59 assists.

Despite the loss, Nevada earned an at-large-bid to the NCAA tournament where it faced Stanford at Maples Pavilion. The Cardinal beat the Pack 3-0, finishing the season 18-13. Three Nevada players received individual honors—Salave'a received First Team All WAC honors, Teal Ericson and Sipherd placed Second Team All-WAC.

igh fliers

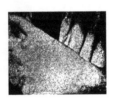

Clockwise from right: Senior Nick **Polinko** dances with sophomore Lauren Robinson during the 2005 All Greek Ball. From left, Theta's, Sara Denton, Jennifer Burke and Shannon **Devreaux** pose with the University of Nevada, Reno Greek Chapter of the Year award following the 2005 All Greek Ball. Delta Delta Delta junior **Aleise** Eberle does her hair before the All Greek Ball Nov. 4. Nevada **Greeks** enjoy dinner at the All Greek Ball Nov. 4 in ballroom at the Circus Circus Hotel Casino in Downtown Reno. Theta junior's Bryana **Shirley** and **Angeline** Peterson show their excitment after their house received Chapter of the Year Award. **K**appa Alpha Theta juniors Angeline Peterson, left, and Lindsey Lee, right, and sophomore Renee Cantu, middle, celebrate after their house received Nevada Greek Chapter of Year honors at the All Greek Ball Nov. 4.

There was formal wear and music, dinner and dancing and for the third straight year, the University of Nevada, Reno Greek Chapter of the Year award was given to UNR's chapter of Kappa Alpha Theta.

Friday night, Nov. 4, when you average student was eating pizza at Pub N' Sub, hundreds of Nevada Greeks gathered at Circus Circus Hotel Casino for the annual All Greek formal Ball.

Clockwise from below: A list of chores hangs inside one of the housing facilities at Washoe County's Kids Kottage. A protective shelter for children. Jennette Ackley, and othe University of Nevada, Reno student volunteers, plays with the children at Kids Kottage. Paul Dente plays red rover with the children at Kids Kottage. Dente holds hands with one of the children during an activity outside.

They played pictionary and charades, drew pictures and made cookies, they even played red rover. Student Orientation Staff and Student Ambassadors spent a day with kids, Saturday, Nov.19, at the Washoe County Kids Kottage. Kids Kottage is a protective shelter where police or social workers bring children after they have been removed from their families. Most children at Kids Kottage are there because their families are suspected of severe abuse or neglect.

"Our groups went to Kids Kottage as a community service," senior Lexi Hughes said. "It's important that organizations do community service. We got to spend time with kids who are having trouble with life right now. These are kids that have been abused and neglected."

"When we first got there I was really nervous," junior Katie Smith said, "but later I got excited. I got to help kids less fortunate than me. I had an incredible feeling that lasted the whole day."

"We got to work with three age groups," sophomore Justin Jo said. "My favorite was the older group. They were willing to play the games and have a good time. The whole day make you feel really good like you were doing more than your part to society. This was a really good community service event for us."

red rover, red

Photos by David Calvert; story by Monika Mala

over

talk about s

Sigma Alpha sister's Sarah Tjoa, Emily Heavrin, Jen Stovall and Victoria Kerrigan brought plenty of dollar bills with them to the Flipside drag show Tuesday night, Nov. 29. The drag show, sponsored by Flipside, was produced by Reno's Silver Dollar Court; proceeds benefited A Rainbow Place—Reno's only LGBT youth center.

The show was a part of Flipside's annual Sexual Awareness week. In addition to the drag queens, the Associated Students of the University of Nevada sponsored an open forum with Moonlight Bunny Ranch Brothel owner Dennis Hof. Hof, and "working girl" Bunny Love defended prostitution and answered the audiences questions.

"People have a bad image of prostitution," Hof said. "They think that prostitution means girls on a street-corner, pimps waiting down the street.... That's not what we do."

Counter-clockwise from left: Emily Heavrin inserts a dollar bill into the shorts of a male dancer during the Flipside sponsored drag show in the Silver and Blue room at Lawlor Events Center, Nov. 29. From left, Sigma Alpha sisters, Sarah Tjoa, Emily Heavrin, Jen Stovall and Victoria Kerrigan cheer during the drag show. Proceeds from the show helped benefit A Rainbow Place. Drag queen, Trixxy, performs at the Flipside drag show at Lawlor Events Center Nov. 29.

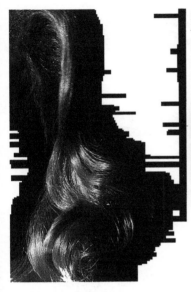

Clockwise from far below: Brothel owner **Dennis Hof** speaks outside the student services building, Wednesday, Dec. 30. Hof discussed prostitution, his work at the Bunny Ranch and the life of a working girl. **He's** got legs. Trixxy performs at the Flipside drag show, Tuesday, Dec. 29. **A drag queen** performs Tuesday night during the drag show. Hof's visit and the drag show were a part of Flipsides's Sexual Awareness Week.

special education

Photos & story by Ben Ragains

Shannon Reynolds is not your average education student. A Special Education and Primary Education dual major Reynolds works three jobs to support her schooling. But one of them is special. Two days a week, Reynolds nannies for Dan and Karin Dixon's 22-month-old son, Kyle. Reynolds says she looks at taking care of Kyle as an opportunity to use and develop the skills she is being taught at UNR.

"It's not like I use Kyle as my own little science experiment, but there's no better way to see knowledge develop, and be a part of that process, than with an amazingly smart little boy," Reynolds said. "There's nobody better to learn from than kids themselves. Kyle gives me a real life education."

Counter clockwise from above: Shannon Reynolds carefully guides Kyle down the slide in the his backyard. Reynolds is a full-time student at the University of Nevada, Reno, studying Special Education and Primary Education. She serves as a part time nanny for Dan and Karin Dixon's 22 month-old boy, named Kyle. Reynolds takes a break from studying to show Kyle some fun games on the Internet. Reynolds smiles while caring for Kyle. Reynolds and Kyle look out into the Dixon's large yard.

artemisia

photo magazine for the University of Nevada, Reno

Iss. Two, Vol. 117, Winter 2005

This issue is sponsored by the following donors:

The Associated Students of the University of Nevada

The Jot Travis Student Union

University Studies Abroad Consortium

Lombardi Recreation

Planned Parenthood

Kaplan

Nevada Fine Arts

Keva Juice of Reno

Lightning Source UK Ltd.
Milton Keynes UK
UKHW010252231118
332756UK00012B/2033/P